D0399259

LETTS GUIDES TO
✧ GARDEN DESIGN ✧

Walls & Screens

LETTS GUIDES TO
✧ GARDEN DESIGN ✧

Walls & Screens

✧ DIANA SAVILLE ✧

CANOPY BOOKS
A Division of Abbeville Publishing Group
NEW YORK LONDON PARIS

First published in the United States in 1994
by Canopy Books, a division of Abbeville Publishing Group
488 Madison Avenue
New York NY 10022

First published in the United Kingdom in 1993
by Charles Letts & Co Ltd.
Letts of London House, Parkgate Road
London SW11 4NQ

Series editor: Diana Saville

Edited, designed and produced by Robert Ditchfield Ltd.
Copyright © Robert Ditchfield Ltd. 1993.

All rights reserved under international copyright conventions.
No part of this book may be reproduced or utilized in any
form or by any means, electronic or mechanical, including
photocopying, recording, or by any information storage and
retrieval system, without permission in writing from the
publisher. Inquiries should be addressed to Abbeville
Publishing Group, 488 Madison Avenue, New York, NY 10022.
Printed and bound in Belgium.

ISBN 1-55859-660-7

A CIP catalogue record for this book is available from the British Library.

ACKNOWLEDGMENTS

Photographs are reproduced by kind permission of the following: Robert Ditchfield
Ltd.: 30 (photographer John Franks) and 2, 49 right (photographer Bob Gibbons)
and 22/23, 39 (photographer Jerry Hardman-Jones/York Gate); W. A. Lord: 10.
All other photographs are by Diana Saville who would like to thank the owners of
the many gardens which include Arrow Cottage (17), Barnsley House (50), 23,
Beechcroft Road, Oxford (13), Bourton House (18/19), Close Farm (27, 46), Garden
of Mr. Milton Grundy (12/13), Hidcote (44/45), Hill Court (32), Hodges Barn (21),
Lower Hall (15), Lower Hope (43 right), Misarden (37 top), Powis Castle (37 bottom,
44, 49 left), Preen Manor (25, 54), The Priory (51), Rous Lench (6), Snowshill (14,
52), Sissinghurst (7, 8, 38, 53), Stone House Cottage (22, 40), The Walled Garden
(61), Westbury Court (56, 57), Woodlands (58), Woodpeckers (60).

ILLUSTRATIONS

Page 1: Tulips and bearded irises hem the foot of a cottage wall.
Frontispiece: Rosa "Anemone"—Chinese in its perfect simplicity—is one of the
earliest climbing roses to flower.
Page 5: Clematis "Elsa Späth."

CONTENTS

LEFT: *Yew is adaptable and long-lived; these ancient hedges tolerate this highly intricate trimming.*

OPPOSITE: *Entwined* Clematis *'Perle d'Azur' and 'Jackmannii Superba'.*

INTRODUCTION

N early everybody has walls in their garden. At the very least, they have one wall of a house, at the most walls within walls. Most of us come somewhere in between with a rectangle of walls or fences around the back of the garden and, often, a little one at the front.

This is no modern development. Rather, walled gardens like this are a link with the past for they are of ancient and almost universal origin. They have provided a cloistered place of refuge and been a form of green and ideal beauty for most of the world's great civilizations. It is scarcely surprising. Gardens protected by walls have a snugness for they give shelter, privacy and protection. Entering their gate you are drawn into a secret, harmonious world of your own in which the nice things are kept in and the nastier things are excluded.

Walled Gardens of the Past

T his may have been still truer of gardens in the past when the outside world was more than just troublesome. Its threat of wild animals and even wilder people was continuous and terrifying. In contrast, within the walled sanctuary, there was a microcosm of enchantment. The Romans, for example, developed an outdoor room that conformed to their notion of comfort and luxury. The Persians, whose gardens were to exercise an extraordinary influence on our own, built ideal forms of gardens within walls. One notable design (sometimes seen also on Persian carpets) was based on a great right-angled cross which symbolized the four quarters of the universe, divided by four large rivers. The walls of these exquisite gardens were occasionally surmounted by narrow beds of flowers, or even embellished with coloured glazed tiles.

Designs of this kind influenced the gardens of Islam and later those of the great Moguls in India. Here the Emperor Babur in the sixteenth century established the *chaharbagh*, a four-fold enclosed garden in the Persian style: for until his conquest of India, the enclosed garden with a strong axial plan did not exist. Indeed, it was he who complained on entering Hindustan not just that it was ugly, nor just that it was on a level plain but that, alas, 'its gardens have not walls'.

A background hedge gives a frame and anchor to this luxuriant planting.

Walls of the Far East

In the Far East, as in the Near, garden walls were considered essential. In China every ingenuity was devised. They held dramatic apertures like shells, fans, keyholes, circles; and the latter (the moongate – in China, the circle symbolizes heaven) was imitated in the West centuries later. The Japanese, too, subjected their walls to the most dextrous variations and if an owner had to move his home, he might dig up not only his trees but his ornamental fence as well.

Walls of the West

In the West, all gardens were also walled for there existed the unthinking acceptance that a garden of any nature should be a simple walled rectangle or a series of linked symmetrical rectangles. In England, this reliance on the enclosure remained unshaken until the eighteenth century and the landscape movement. Only then did the throwing down of walls take place and the break with the universal mainstream tradition of the enclosure.

More than a century was to pass before the yearning reawoke for the old enclosed formal gardens of England. So, now once again, boundaries mattered – whether of quiet yew hedges or walls of masonry. Scrupulous attention, for example, was paid to wall decorations by the architects with whom Gertrude Jekyll worked. Pinnacle tops, balustrading, buttresses, walls with openwork panels, parapets of curved tiles, walls covered with tiled ridges, dry stone walls, walls patterned with intricate arrangements of stone on stone, brick on brick – all these had their part to play in the overall pattern of the garden.

The Importance of Plants

But it wasn't just walls that mattered. Plants did too. At a time when horticultural material had flooded in from the plant hunters' expeditions, a new emphasis was placed on vegetable life. The walls were brought dazzlingly to life. A spillage of creepers and festoons of flowers were meticulously added so that the highlights of the walls were embellished, not insensitively obliterated. The gardens of this time were the virtuoso product of horticulturalist and architect in a way that had never happened before.

It has not happened on this scale either since then. Looking back from today, it is startling to realise that, for most of the twentieth century, we have lost this great adventurousness with walls and their plants. Perhaps we are just beginning to recapture it, to realize again how important this vertical dimension is to our little gardens. How its space can be architecturally explored and enhanced with plants. How much opportunity it gives for growing in layers – one plant upon a supporting host, so that they will flower together in an entrancing combination or successively to extend the season of blossom in the garden.

It is worth, too, recapturing the sheer variety of walls that were part of gardens, each with its own special character. The low drystone walls, ornamental fences and trelliswork, the retaining walls of a bank turned into a crinoline of flowers with their bouffant profile, even the crinkle-crankle walls that swooped in and out so that fruit could grow in the snug nooks of their undulations.

Nor should one ever forget hedges, the most glorious and often underrated elements in the garden. Hedges make walls, too, in a garden. Any enclosure bounded by the high, rigid lines of clipped yew is as effective as a walled area: its boundaries are quite as opaque and certainly as impenetrable. Its top-knots of fantastical topiary can be every bit as ingenious as the pinnacles of a hard stone wall or the capping on a trellis.

Planting at the wall top meets that at its foot; the golden alyssum here provides the link.

Permanence: the Lesson of the Past

What one must always remember is that hedges, like walls, are the most important features in a garden. The past teaches us this. Its lesson is that hedges and walls are the elements that give a greater degree of stability and permanence than any other furniture in a garden. They resemble large trees in this respect. They are like them, too, in the degree of commitment they imply from us. And like trees, too, in that they stand a chance of lasting long into the future, just as they have stretched so very far back into the past.

9

THE PURPOSES OF WALLS

If you assess the purpose of walls and screens, you find that they tend to fall into three main categories of use. In the first, the wall acts as an element of design. To the garden architect, for example, the prime purpose of a wall or fence is to shape an area and to dictate its size. It also gives a feeling of permanence and solidity to the landscape, ensuring that a garden looks substantial rather than a flimsy entity doomed to evaporate in the winter and renew itself in spring.

In the second category, the wall is exploited as a horticultural asset. The keen gardener will view it as a picturesque way of growing climbers or tender plants. The former need its support over which they will drape, lean, hook or shove their way upwards towards light. Tender plants also require the comfort of a wall, in the lee of which they stand a better chance of surviving a cold winter as their wood is ripened by the wall's warmth.

The third main purpose of a wall or fence is to act as a barrier, whether against prying neighbours, hideous eyesores or, literally, intruders like rioting animals or children. Even an owner who takes a passive attitude towards his garden will appreciate the privacy, security and shelter that his walls or screens should provide.

Matching the Wall to its Function

These, then, are the main purposes of walls and it is absolutely essential that you are clear which of the functions you want your own wall to perform. This is true whether it is to fulfil just one purpose or whether it should

A pattern of low hedges and cones set within a framework of tall hedges shapes this formal garden which looks as elegant in winter as in summer.

Tender plants like cistus benefit from the warm micro-climate beside the tall wall of a house.

be useful on all fronts. If you omit to sort this out, you may risk selecting the wrong type of wall, or failing to exploit successfully the wall you already possess.

On pages 16–25, I give an idea of the various types of walls or screens you can choose. Some can be erected within a few days, others such as slow-growing hedges will take years to reach maturity. Solid walls may cause turbulent gusts; in contrast, openwork screens will diffuse and reduce wind, thereby increasing shelter not only for you but for your plants. Such walls create micro-climates and it is the favourable kind that the gardener relishes for wind and cold are the enemies of his plants.

Micro-climates

The owner of an area made snug and warm by walls discovers the astonishing differ-ence it makes to the kinds of plants he can grow. It benefits not only those in the immedi-ate lee of shelter but the plants seemingly beyond its reach. In such circumstances, the gardener can develop an area of Mediterranean luxuriance. Scent, too, will linger here, the more intense for being trapped within the enclosure. This is one example of the way that your choice and placing of a wall will actually govern the kind of plants you grow, the lavishness of your effects, the scents you sniff, the permanence of your planting and, not least, the degree of comfort in which you view them – for you, like they, can sit within a sheltered nook. All of you are benefiting from the micro-climate that a wall can provide, which will differ from elsewhere in the garden. This is not merely seasonal, but a year-round asset. For the fragile blossoms of winter-flowering plants will be more gently preserved in the extra shelter, and the leaves of evergreens less likely to suffer from frost.

11

ASPECTS OF DESIGN

*T*here are so many beautiful and unexpected possibilities presented by walls and screens that a positive *embarras de choix* threatens. However, the size and locality of a garden limits its owner's options and forces certain decisions. A crucial point, for example, is whether the wall or screen should act as a total obliterator – namely, one which blinkers you against the rest of your garden and the outside world. Or whether it is more useful as a partial obstruction, so that your eye is channelled along a certain view. Secondly, is a formal or informal effect more suitable? Finally, what kind of shape do you want to create with your screen? This may mean thinking, too, about its knock-on effects. What of the shadows it creates? The change of balance in the rest of the garden?

The purpose of your wall will in many cases make the decision for you – and that, in turn, will probably depend on where you live.

The Little Courtyard

*I*n a city, especially, gardens match the original meaning of a yard – an enclosure surrounded by walls. These define its shape and its extent. In a very small area, further sub-division may not be desirable though

low walls and hedges will help to turn it into a pattern. This will add interest and individuality in the same way that features do to a face.

Such patterns are usually formal. In most cases, one welcomes the lines of the boundary, be they square or rectangular, by reinforcing them further with straight lines. A similarly formal but softer effect is achieved by the use of an inner circle or oval, perhaps again provided by low curved walls within the area. An octagon is sometimes preferred and this (or the circle) can be used as a frame for a raised bed or to hold water providing a formal decorative pool.

Another treatment for the courtyard is to break up its space with asymmetrical focal points. No one has more to teach us in this respect than the Japanese whose courtyard gardens (called *tsuboniwa*) are models of asymmetrical formality and restraint. They don't forget the value of empty space as a shape in itself and, in short, show us the wisdom of not attempting too much in a small area.

In contrast the Chinese treatment of a courtyard may involve dividing the area into yet smaller spaces by screens and walls. Paradoxically this may give the effect of more space. Apertures in one or more of these walls allow framed glimpses of what lies

beyond. Walls painted palest grey recede and disappear into the background. Trees allowed to grow high and overhang the confines of their cell will dispel a feeling of claustrophobia.

A third treatment is possible in tiny gardens and is the most appealing to the romantic and plant enthusiast. Although you can never lose your boundaries in an area of this size, you might use them as a means of smothering

yourself with foliage and flowers. Layer upon layer will give you total privacy, muffling nearby sounds, surrounding you with the vitality of plant life.

ABOVE: *Walled moss garden in the Japanese style demonstrating that there is a value in not cluttering empty space.*

RIGHT: *The boundaries of this tiny city garden have been camouflaged with plants, a device that appears to enlarge it.*

13

OPPOSITE: *The fence beyond the arch limits your view. The interest derives instead from the colour match of the flowers.*

The Long Garden

Where disproportionate length and narrowness are problems, it is walls, fences and hedges which provide the solution. You can use these to divide the garden into self-contained sections – most obviously by slicing the length several times across at right-angles, with or without corridors. If you are going to use two or more of these divisons, you can make alluring through-views by lining up various openings or doors. These were once coyly called garden peeps.

Less simple cross-structures would involve devising curved or even triangular divisons but these have the disadvantage of looking designer-led (imposed from a pattern-book) in a small area.

The result of dividing the long and narrow area is that you end up with a series of linked enclosed gardens rather in the medieval manner. The great virtue of this enclosure system is that it conceals what you don't wish to show (rubbish, say) and also prevents you from absorbing and thereby exhausting your whole garden in one glance. If you are untroubled by this last point, then you could use a low wall or hedge. These could also act as cross-structures dividing length, yet permit you to watch, for example, a child's activities.

The path leads you to the doorway and beyond, relieving the claustrophobia that is inherent in every walled garden.

The Larger Garden

The larger garden with walls is often in the country. It may differ from its town cousins in that the land beyond its walls is actually worth seeing. This presents a challenge. How best to use a wall which emphatically excludes your view. One early device was the inclusion of a grille or railings in a section of the wall. Its equivalent nowadays is a see-through gate or even a solid door, propped ajar – which is just as effective and always inviting. Alternatively, in some hedges you can make windows and doors by cutting openings in the branches and arching the shrub over. The selection of hedges on page 21 gives some idea of those that are good-tempered enough to put up with this type of punishment.

A large country garden also lends itself to repeated sub-division by hedges and the famous example of this is at Hidcote Manor in Gloucestershire. It is its little 'rooms' which have earned it popular acclaim, but the genius of its construction lies rather in its use of the axial line (formed by hornbeam hedges) which takes the eye to the distance where the view climaxes in the world outside the garden. That prevents this garden of multiple sub-divisions from causing claustrophobia. This axial line at Hidcote is a straight one. But anyone putting in hedges for this purpose should note that, even in a smallish garden, one can plant a corridor of hedges so that they form converging rather than parallel lines. This will ensure that the corridor seems even longer.

Hawthorn forms an upper layer to the stone wall, providing greater privacy. It is trimmed in steps for interest and bulges over the wall beneath which ensures a comfortable clothed effect.

THE CHOICE
OF WALLS

Walls are either living or artificial. They are formed by hedges; or by masonry (or wood) of some kind. Both categories are durable, both form effective boundaries and barriers, both secure privacy, shelter and, probably, shade on one side and sun on the other. What, then, are the pros and cons of the two kinds?

The most obvious argument in favour of a constructed wall is that it comes rapidly into existence. By contrast even the quickest growing hedge will make you wait for your privacy and shelter; it is useless until fully established.

Also, hedges need maintenance now and forever. They have to be weeded when young. They must be clipped from one to three times a year (depending on variety) which is an

important point if you plan to retire or reduce labour. They also tend to outgrow their station over a number of years, growing ever wider and becoming corpulent, even obese, in maturity. And when used as shared boundaries with neighbours, your neighbour and his successor must cooperate in cutting his side. So one is bound to conclude that hedges, like all living organisms, bring problems that temper their merits.

On the other hand most are cheaper by far than walls. They are good at merging self-effacingly into a country landscape. They are equally good at holding the stage and giving the garden a stamp of its own. A garden can be made memorable by the use of hedges alone. Indeed certain hedges convey such dignity and drama that they add up to a far greater asset than the sum of their problems.

On the more practical side, the provision of shelter is vital in a garden, especially a new one. In this respect, hedges score highly over solid walls. The latter provoke tremendous turbulence and eddying, particularly on the side of the prevailing wind. Put an open doorway in the wall and you can expose yourself to a scourging wind, the more lethal for being channelled through a narrow gap. A high established hedge, however, will act as a wind filter and reduce the violence of the onslaught.

This is one advantage that is similarly offered by openwork walls – rather in the form of brick screens instead of the crudely patterned ornamental concrete blocks – and the best wind filter is achieved by a proportion of 60% of solid material to 40% apertures. Semi-permeable fences and decorative trellis will also act as wind filters, though the degree of privacy they offer may be limited.

The Plain Brick Wall

The high plain brick wall can be one of the glories of the garden. It is also relatively easy to build as the units are light, of uniform size and simple to cut. However, the kind of bricks matters a great deal. New ones (with certain exceptions) can look flashy, especially in front of an old brick house. Second-hand bricks are preferable though it is essential they are weathered or they will start to flake and crumble at the first sign of frost.

The choice of bonding (the pattern in which the bricks are laid) is also important. So is the treatment of the joints. The mortar can be flush with the surface, raked out or scooped back (keyed) which makes the bricks project obtrusively. A damp-proof course is the subject of furious if local debate. There is no controversy about coping; this is essential on all solid walls to prevent the entry of rain.

An open-work brick screen is decorative and substantial and more efficient at slowing and reducing wind than its solid counterpart. Although it cannot provide total privacy, a clothing of plants will improve this.

An openwork brick screen filters wind much more effectively than a solid wall which dams currents and sets up turbulence.

The Stone Wall

The natural stone wall quickly weathers to the look of a cherished antique. It needs to be built by a good craftsman and merits the same respect as any capable artist's product. Sun-warmed, lichened and colonized by plants and animals, it acquires a private life you can only guess at. Plants blend into it unobtrusively and you rarely get the frenzied colour-fights that are so alarming on a brick wall planted with a

rose like 'Danse du Feu'. As with the brick wall, the joints matter: the best finish is for the mortar to be marginally less than flush with the stone and, of course, brushed away from the surface.

The Ornamental Screen-block

This kind of screen was actually championed by Gertrude Jekyll early this century in *Gardens for Small Country Houses* where she

commended its 'light and lacy effects' (moulded brick rather than concrete was used in the example she showed). The trouble is that its use today in so many un- or ill-designed, crudely planted gardens has led to noxious associations. The other disadvantage is that you are buying in a manufacturer's moulded patterned blocks when making such a wall, and the monotony of this repeated pattern throughout the wall is a curse. One cannot recommend it, but if

ABOVE: *Climbing roses including the sumptuous recurrent-flowering 'Iceberg' smother railings in a front garden.*

OPPOSITE: *Trellis used as divider. It is sturdy enough to give an architectural backdrop to the herbaceous border, but softened by a curving top and decorative capping.*

you have one already, a full-blooded drapery of plants will transform it.

Trellis

Here one has an immensely adaptable device, for it can be erected as a free-standing screen or nailed firmly to a low existing wall to increase its height. In the case of the latter, the join will be largely concealed by plants when established. Trellis has an ancient and honourable history: it was inventively used in medieval gardens, embossed with flowers, and had become all the rage by the seventeenth century. It is an admirable wind filter, and gives shade when densely festooned with ample-leafed climbers. It is equally decorative when used unclothed, making a stronger ornamental statement about the garden than its other wooden relative, the fence.

Fences

These are relatively cheap, wind-filtering and suppliers of privacy. Wattle blends well in a garden but other mass-produced, wooden fences are not always decorative and may be better used as invisible plant supports, clad perhaps in ivy to provide an evergreen background to richly coloured climbers piled on top. Split chestnut palings, linked with wires, and ranch-type fencing – usually painted white though a dark green wood stain would be a nice alternative – are both attractive though less effective screens than the solid fence. If they are partly clothed in climbers, this will increase their usefulness as shelter-belts. In all these cases, the fencing-posts need to be strong and securely set in the ground, preferably in concrete.

Low picket fences and decorative metalwork fences of the last century (whose designs have more in common with trelliswork) have both charm and elegance. A front garden, its flowers frothing forwards through their corset of railings, can look especially enticing.

LEFT: *Chaenomeles is clipped after flowering in spring to form a brilliant floriferous hedge the following year.*

OPPOSITE: *This perfect tapestry hedge is formed of yew, holly, beech and Lawson's cypress (the ratio of deciduous plants to evergreen is 1:3). Clipping should take account of the different rates of growth within such a hedge.*

LIVING WALLS: HEDGES

We tend to undervalue hedges. For decades we have regarded them as self-effacing workhorses in the garden, instead of as structures which have ornamental value in themselves. Their worthy functions – keeping out stock and intruders, securing privacy, saying this land belongs to me – have obscured their decorative potential. Yet they can be used in the most varied ways as adornment. They make avenues, internal divisions, low as well as high walls, knot gardens and frames for features like a seat or a sculpture. Hedges can be planted in circles, serpentine or curving lines, or on their own clear stems as stilt hedges or sweeping to the ground as usual. They can be tapestried (formed of different species of varying colours), they can be crisply formal or trimmed into interesting bulges: they can have buttresses or orna-

mental trimmings like crenellations, spheres, squares, cones, birds and pediments. A hedge can be sculpted or, in contrast, make an informal billowy flowering line.

Hedge possibilities are numerous. How does one choose? This depends on where you live, the type of soil in the garden, the purpose for which you need a hedge, the height you want and the room you have for its width. It depends too on the time you will wait for its maturity, how often you are willing to clip it, whether you want an evergreen or a deciduous shrub, whether you want it to flower or fruit. Your needs may narrow the choice to a few only of these possibilities.

A less easily definable factor than any of the above is the effect you want to achieve. What I can only call the look and feel of the beast comes into it, for hedges are so much more than utilitarian. Certain types have a peculiar decorative charm and their old or modern associations may give a dominant flavour to the garden.

The body form of a hedge will alter its effect, too, just as it does with thin and fat people. A hedge can be grown like the profile of a Gothic church spire: very slim, soaring and tapering to a near whisker. Or it can be given a substantial, mature appearance, achieved by the use of a batter (the slope to which the hedge's sides are cut) which narrows very gently until about three-quarters of the way up, then less gently into a slightly rounded top. This gives a more homely, old-fashioned air. Not all hedges adapt to all treatments, but some of the most useful are listed opposite.

Varieties of Hedge
(Planting distances given in brackets.
E = Evergreen.)

Beech (*Fagus sylvatica*) makes probably the best formal deciduous hedge and will grow on any soil so long as it is well-drained. It is wind-resistant and tolerates a polluted atmosphere. Its fresh green leaves turn russet in autumn and if the hedge is given its annual clip in late summer, it will keep these leaves throughout the winter, making it a year-round screen. It lends itself to being trained into doorways etc., even topiaried. Copper beech is sometimes blended with it to give variegation, or used on its own though its effect is puddingy. (18in/45cm).

Box (E) *Buxus sempervirens* is found on chalk in the wild, but thrives on almost any well-drained soil and is good in sun or partial shade. It is splendid for high formal hedges up to 8ft/2.4m or more and the most robust cultivar, 'Handsworthensis', will reach to some 15ft/4.6m. It is a good subject for topiary, and has a rich musty scent that rolls over you like a fog in an enclosed area. The

roots can be invasive. (18in/45cm). See page 38 for its low-growing relative, *B. sempervirens* 'Suffruticosa'.

Chaenomeles Certain cultivars make a brilliant flowering hedge in spring and the hard clipping of the shrub after blossoming will encourage its floriferousness. 'Rowallane' (a rich coral), 'Pink Lady' or 'Moerloosei' (pink and white) would all make a medium-height hedge to a maximum of 5ft/1.5m. (18in/45cm).

Chamaecyparis lawsoniana (E) This used to be highly popular and is good in windy places and in shade. The green of the type is dull when clipped formally; it is more attractive when grown as a free informal screen, showing its varying tones as it ripples in the wind. There are many cultivars of different shades from blue to bright green to gold and also some of slower-growing habit, such as 'Fletcheri', which relieves you of frequent clipping. (2ft/60cm).

Hawthorn *Crataegus monogyna* will grow anywhere and on any soil and is thorny, tough, wind- and stock-resistant and blends into its surroundings. Its surface has been

21

likened to a fine tweed and its twigginess means that it can be trimmed satisfactorily into apertures: indeed it was one of the first subjects used for arbours and is highly adaptable. To be stock-proof, it must be planted in two staggered rows. As tall as you like, or lowish. (12in/30cm).

Holly (E) A dependable hedge in any but a cold continental-type climate. It has a glittering surface to its leaves and is reliable in either sun or shade. Spiny leaves are agonizing to encounter. Try instead the spineless *Ilex* × *altaclarensis* 'Camelliifolia' or the hardly toothed *I. aquifolium* 'J.C. van Thol'.

Slowish-growing (with exceptions) to 20ft/ 6m. (18in/45cm).

Hornbeam *Carpinus betulus* forms a strong, dense hedge resembling beech for which it is usually substituted on cold wet soils. It also retain its donkey brown leaves in winter in sheltered areas, so can act as a year-round screen although deciduous. Can be cut into arches and apertures. It will grow to 20ft/ 6m and still retain its density. (18in/45cm).

Myrobalan *Prunus cerasifera* is quick to make effect but needs clipping three times a year. It flowers freely in early spring, white in the type or pale pink in its claret-leafed form

'Pissardii' or the even darker 'Nigra'. In a formal garden, these hedges can make pretty backgrounds to borders of pink, cream or lavender flowers. Up to 10ft/3m. (2 – 3ft/60 – 90cm).

Thuja plicata (E) A quick-growing conifer with mat dark green scales known as the Western Red Cedar which will need clipping twice a year. Its foliage has a sweet, quite spicy smell. Makes a good dense hedge to 16ft/4.8m. *Thuja occidentalis* forms an equally good dense hedge and is slower-growing. (2ft/60cm).

Yew (E) *Taxus baccata* is superior to all its rivals. Velvety, dark, light-absorbent, it makes the best background to garden flowers. It tolerates any amount of cutting back and architectural shaping. 'Hicksii', a hybrid raised from *T.* × *meadia*, is one of the hardiest cultivars in severe conditions. Two warnings: don't plant on water-logged soils, nor where stock can be poisoned by it. (18in/45cm).

ABOVE LEFT: *Unusually slim profile on a pair of yew hedges.*

ABOVE RIGHT: *The endlessly adaptable yew again, cut to a symmetry of peaks, joined at the base.*

LIVING SCREENS

A loose, living screen of unclipped trees or shrubs gives a different feeling to a garden. It is at the opposite extreme from the dark and severe architecture of formal hedges. It grows freely, enjoying the licence of throwing its stems around, rather than being carved into a rectangular block. This means that, even when planted along geometric lines, its profile will always be relaxed.

This informality may be just what you want. However, it does require careful positioning. Such a screen should be an ornament in itself. Plant it in its own right, rather than as a companion-piece. It makes an inferior background, for example, to a flower border whose confusion and variety has to be corseted by a trim, carved surround.

A screen may give you more privacy at some times than others. Lots of the best subjects are deciduous which means they will be ineffective in winter. On the other hand, they will make as strong a block as any proper hedge in summer – maybe better since most screens are allowed to grow to their natural height and spill forwards on the ground. The result of this is that many will occupy a lot of space, possibly more than you can allow.

So long as the screen conforms coherently to the style of its setting, one can go bush, Japanese or romantic. One can plant for scent, colour or form. A garden I know has a short avenue of white philadelphus – dull-leafed perhaps but a triumphal avalanche in summer when it produces its cascade of white, intensely scented blossom. The white and scented themes could be explored with white rugosa roses, producing a succession all summer of large, single, simple flowers of the greatest purity.

White is safe. Other colours should be judged for their dazzle-factor: a line of egg-yolk yellow would be too unyielding for a garden to absorb. With a flowering hedge, consider too the proportion of flowers to leaves, which will have a serious effect on the saturation of colour. All-over floriferousness can be oppressive.

Other screens commend themselves for their natural shapeliness. They may not have flowers as their chief attraction: it is the elegance of their form that is winning. Bamboos and grasses make wonderful foliage screens for this reason.

Free-growing screen of rugosa roses. These sucker if grown on their own roots, which ensures a bushy hedge at the bottom.

Japanese flavour, achieved by a combination of hard pebbles and a soft flexible screen of bamboos.

Select List of Candidates

***A**rundinaria murieliae* (E) Most decorative clump-forming bamboo with narrow green leaves on arching canes to 10ft/3m. Forms a dense thicket of canes which age from rich green to yellow. 'Simba' is a more compact form.

Camellia (E) For acid, humus-rich, well-drained but moist soil only in cool temperate regions. For an expensive informal tall screen, consider the columnar 'E.G. Waterhouse' with pale pink formal double flowers in spring (for sun); or the white anemone form 'Mary Costa'. 10ft/3m plus.

***Miscanthus* 'Silver Feather'** Grass with fountain of green leaves and silky silver flower plumes in autumn. 7ft/2.1m. *M. sacchariflorus* is a bit taller. Both die down in winter.

Roses make beautiful flowering screens. Encourage them to be bushy at the base by cutting them hard back in the spring after planting. Of the rugosa roses, try 'Scabrosa' with single magenta flowers and large hips (5ft/1.5m); 'Roseraie de l'Hay', double crimson-purple, very scented (up to 7ft/2.1m). Perfumed hybrid musks include the pink 'Cornelia', blush 'Penelope' and apricot 'Buff Beauty' (5ft/1.4m). The Alba roses are tough and dependable; try the scented, shell pink, cupped 'Celestial' with glaucous leaves (6ft/1.8m). 'Nevada' is the glory of the moderns with large creamy semi-double blooms and small species-type foliage; 7ft/2.1m.

Sinarundinaria nitida (E) Bamboo like *A. murieliae* but daintier and a deeper green. Needs shelter from wind and in winter. 12ft/3.6m.

Tamarix pentandra Gauzy, soft, feathery glaucous foliage on wiry stems and pink flower sprays (rosy-red in 'Rubra') in late summer. *T. tetrandra* has darker foliage and pink flowers in late spring. For sun and good drainage which will increase hardiness. 10ft/3m.

LEFT: Clematis viticella *'Etoile Violette'* scrambles through the climbing rose *'New Dawn'*.

OPPOSITE: The spring-flowering Ceanothus *'Cascade'* has gracefully pendulous growth.

CLIMBERS AND SHRUBS FOR THE HIGH WALL

Planting the high wall is exacting. Putting the right plant in the right place is more important on walls than elsewhere in the garden. A grown-up climber is not as mobile as its little relative in the border and some are so permanent that they can outlive their owner. Errors in planting are therefore rather more than just costly. They are a curse in terms of time as a replacement plant may take years to cover the space and bulk into a substantial presence.

Every feature of the plant needs to be considered, from its liking for a particular soil and aspect to its method of growth, to its ultimate size and its flower and leaf habit. Size is crucial and before you lift a trowel, you have to check out the space available and the plant's likely growth in relation to its position. The importance of flower habit is that it makes some plants more suitable for walls than elsewhere. For example, plants which deserve a prominent position against a high wall include the taller kinds which have pendulous flowers; their pensive grace will be advantageously displayed in this position.

Scenic Design

With a large area to plant, you have to think in more general terms too. As is true of almost every aspect of landscape design, you are planting in order to conceal or to display (or emphasize). In general one needs climbers to redeem an ugly building or wall, highlight a good one and display their own perfections, probably at a stud-ied time of the year. In addition, there are plenty of things you don't want them to do – to infest low-slung eaves, block gutters, lift tiles, obscure windows, conceal handsome stonework or push over a fence. All climbers and wall shrubs, no matter how pretty or evocative, are only part of the whole picture.

This is especially true when one comes to plant a house wall, a challenging location which is dealt with in more detail on page 47. Often only the simplest of dressings will fit around doors and windows. And even when one comes to plant large garden walls which allow much more room to let rip, one still has to see climbers in relation to their background.

Climbers and wall shrubs also have to be considered in relation to each other. They are not just individuals: their charm comes as much from their association with their neighbours. No one would doubt the truth of this when assembling herbaceous plants, but the rule is easy to forget when planting high wall subjects, simply because they are giants.

Abutilon × suntense *and* Clematis montana *'Grandiflora' (above left) and the rose 'Madame Grégoire Staechelin' and* Wisteria floribunda *(above right). Both these partnerships look ravishing but the clematis and wisteria will have to be firmly pruned or they will smother their hosts if allowed to grow unchecked.*

Planting in Layers

One of the most attractive ways of associating plants is to grow them in layers. In a tiny garden it is the only way to introduce diversity. With this method you use one plant as a host for another – a fixed marriage and, actually, the same rules pertain to plants as to people. For a life-long union, the two partners should enjoy the same conditions, have complementary characters and appearance and respect each other's need to breathe.

Such partnerships happen in the wild, though the host plant may not always survive its rape by the captor. When it is successful, however, it can provide one of the most spectacular of natural effects.

Good Partners

The way in which climbing plants support themselves explains why some are

potentially such good partners, whereas the touch of others is the kiss of death. Some, like clematis, use twining leaf stems; some, like Virginia creeper, have adhesive pads at the end of their tendrils; some, like honeysuckle, have twining stems; some, such as brambles and roses, use the spines on their long arching shoots to hook into or over whatever they have reached; and others, though not actually climbers, will shove and lean their way up walls in the manner of *Cotoneaster horizontalis*. These groups will provide both hosts and guests, and in some cases, the same plant will be accom- modating in either role (e.g. the rose), depending on its partner.

What you want is a robust, mature host whether its strength lies in its smothering foliage and self-supporting habit (ivy, say) or its thick woody framework (roses and many shrubs such as pyra- cantha, ceanothus, conifers).

Over these can be grown the lanky twining or scrambling kind of plants like clematis or solanums. And even if these clingers turn out to be stranglers in disguise, they can in theory be controlled before their supporter is throttled to death or borne to the ground.

Some of the prettiest effects of growing wall plants in layers can be achieved by the appearance of a delicate light flower against a dark background. In such a case you are not just using the host shrub in its off-season as a sort of bamboo or wire frame, but rather for its type of foliage. As an illustration, a pale-flowered small species clematis allowed to clamber over ivy on a dark and otherwise unpromising wall will look like spangles. Or *Solanum jasminoides album* will form a garland on a yew buttress.

Nor is there any reason why the number of plants should be confined to two; so long as they continue to thrive and don't have to compete too strenuously for the same patch of ground, air and light, you can grow three on top of each other. Say, Virginia creeper as the background for a dark red climbing rose with the white *Clematis* 'Madame Le Coultre' on top of that.

In order to create effects of flowery abundance, you need to know which climbers and wall shrubs bloom simultaneously. You could, for example, plant the spring-flowering *Ceanothus* 'Delight' with the lilac-pink and striped *Clematis* 'Nelly

The down-pipe problem: here golden ivy makes a decorative improvement.

Moser'. This is a mild combination, unlikely to stir the adrenalin. One of spicier intensity would be the ruby velvet climbing rose 'Étoile de Hollande' with *Solanum crispum* 'Glasnevin', a scrambler which would smother the rose with its clustered mauve flower-heads. The combination of leaf and flower-colours can be as powerful: for aplomb, try the black-leafed vine, *Vitis vinifera* 'Purpurea', with the white everlasting pea, *Lathyrus latifolius* 'White Pearl'.

Winter Displays

Summer extravagance cannot be allowed to peter out in winter. At this season, unclothed walls have all the charm of an unlit stove: distinctly chilling. To avoid this, you have to include a high proportion of robust and reliable evergreens on your walls. Spread them around. Clustering them will waste their usefulness as clothing plants in winter. Ivies are one of the main indispensables among the evergreens. These are not boring, as they are now obtainable in lots of speckled, crinkled and variegated forms and many of the most desirable plain green cultivars have handsome architecturally shaped leaves.

Evergreens don't have to be climbers to do an effective job: a broken line or bays of evergreen shrubs against the wall will be just as good. Many of these are not merely serviceable but have such flower glamour that they will take over the starring role in spring and summer.

Camellia japonica 'Nobilissima', an erect robust shrub, is one of the earliest to flower of its group.

A NOTE ABOUT THE FOLLOWING PLANTS

The climbers and wall shrubs that follow are not separated into different categories (though their habit of growth does differ and requires separate training – see page 60). Instead, the plants are presented together in accordance with their main season of display. Some of the plants are tender: a wall is a wonderful opportunity to try those non-hardy but often voluptuously lovely plants which will benefit from its shelter.

Winter Flowers

(E = Evergreen. Explanation of clematis pruning codes A – D = see Page 60).

Camellia (E)   The cultivar 'Narumi-gata' (the most reliable of the winter-blooming species

C. sasanqua) has scented cupped blush-white flowers. 'Nobilissima' is the earliest in bloom of the C. japonica varieties, its great white peony-flowered heads starting in late winter. For moist humus-rich lime-free soil and semi-shade. 10 – 16ft/3 – 4.8m.

Clematis balearica (E)   Climber with nodding heads of greenish-flowers, maroon-spotted within, and delicately scented. Cut foliage bronzing in winter. Vigorous to 16ft/4.8m (D)

Garrya elliptica (E)   Glaucous shrub with clusters of long silver-grey catkins like icicles. Seek out the clone 'James Roof' or at least a male plant as the catkins are longer than those on a female. 10ft/3m.

Ivies (E)   The best include *Hedera helix* 'Hamilton' with 4in/10cm green architectural leaves and sometimes lighter margins; and the slower-growing 'Buttercup' with 2.5in/6cm fully golden new leaves for a semi-shaded corner. All are self-supporting.

Jasminum nudiflorum The ubiquitous winter jasmine doesn't need a wall but is often given

Clematis montana *'Tetrarose' growing through* Actinidia chinensis.

one for the sake of its small starry golden flowers which can spoil in an exposed position. 6ft/1.8m.

Mahonia lomariifolia (E) Elegant shrub like a multi-stemmed dwarf tree, each stem crowned by fronds of tough, prickly leaves, tipped with tufts of lightly scented yellow flowers. 8ft/2.4m.

Pyracantha coccinea 'Lalandei' (E) is a lusty shrub with orange-red autumn-winter fruits following its white flowers in summer. *P. atalantioides* 'Aurea' is equally robust to 20ft/6.5m but has yellow berries. Looks good

with a garrya when it is in catkin, or a golden ivy.

Spring

Abutilon × suntense (Semi-E) Ravishing vigorous shrub with clear violet flowers like 2.5in/6cm saucers (darker in the form 'Jermyns') produced in late spring on a warm wall. Downy grey-green leaves. Sun and good drainage. Not long-lived but very quick to 8ft/2.4m.

Camellia (E) Lankier camellias can have

Magnolia × soulangeana 'Lennei' can be allowed to bush out from the wall as here or, more unusually, trained flat against it.

their long limbs stretched out on walls: these include the pink formal double 'Waterlily', the single pale pink 'J.C. Williams' and the large semi-double, rosy-crimson flowered 'Francie L'. Bushier but upright growers are better planted as free-standing subjects; try 'Bow Bells' with pink, hose-in-hose, bell flowers; or 'Inspiration' with semi-double deep pink blossoms. For shady walls and lime-free soils. To 10ft/3m plus.

Ceanothus (Spring-flowering varieties: E) The finest blue shrubs, best represented by the richly coloured C. *impressus* 'Puget's Blue', by the pendulus 'Cascade', by 'Delight' with paler smoky-blue flowers in panicles; and by 'Concha', a strong blue, which is rather tenderer though all need wall protection to survive in cooler regions. Very vigorous to 10ft/3m and as much across. Full sun.

Chaenomeles needs firm training and hard pruning to flower neatly and well on a wall. C. × *superba* 'Pink Lady' is dependable: C. *speciosa* 'Nivalis' has smaller white flowers that can spangle dark corners in a garden; those of 'Moerloosei' are like pink and white apple-blossom. To 6ft/1.8m.

Clematis armandii with tiny starry white blossoms is the only evergreen of the spring-flowering varieties; 20ft/6m. The best of *C. alpina* include 'Willy' (icy pink), 'Frances Rivis', cobalt blue, and 'Ruby', greyish-purple; all have nodding 1.5in/3cm bells; to 8ft/2.4m. *C. macropetala*, with semi-double bells, flowers in late spring; the richest deep blue form, 'Maidwell Hall' is enchanting mingled with the rosy cultivar 'Markham's Pink'; 10ft/3m. The vanilla-scented *C. montana* is the season's giant grower; 'Alexander' is a good white, *C.m. rubens* a pale pink with bronze foliage, whilst 'Tetrarose' has larger 3in/7.5cm saucer flowers of a good lilac-pink. 20ft/6m or more. (All D).

Magnolia Few are suitable for walls, an exception being *M. × soulangeana* 'Lennei' with deep purple-rose goblet flowers; its long stems, flexible in youth, can be stretched back on supports. 'Picture' with huge crimson-purple flowers, white and waxen within, can also be trained. They give an air of cossetted luxury to their area, but as their great blooms appear on naked branches, grow ivy behind them on the wall. For sun and best in lime-free soil. 20ft/6m high and wide but can be pruned after flowering to much less.

Rose For very late spring, try the lovely *R.* 'Anemone' (syn. *R. anemonoides*), a large single pink of the purest simplicity; 12ft/4m. Or the semi-evergreen *R. banksia* 'Lutea', delicate yet magnificent for a huge area, with double primrose rosettes festooning its stems like garlands; to 40ft/13m. Sun and shelter for both.

Wisteria floribunda 'Multijuga' is unsurpassed in its genus for the length of its fragrant lilac-purple racemes up to 3ft/1m or more. The white 'Alba' though shorter is as noble, a must for excessive effects. 27ft/8m. *W. sinensis* has stubbier racemes, those of the cultivar 'Caroline' an especially rich violet. Sun essential and don't overfeed if slow to flower. 60ft/18.5m.

Summer

Actinidia kolomikta Decorative foliage on

Carpenteria californica, *lovely but tender without wall protection in cold areas.*

twining climber at its best in early summer. Its 6in/15cm green leaves terminate in a creamy and pink portion. Shelter, best in sun. Up to 20ft/6m.

Carpenteria californica (E) A beautiful shrub with pure, refined white flowers bossed with a centre of yellow stamens, like a single rose. Narrow dark leaves with a glaucous underside. For full sun, shelter, soil with sand and humus. To about 6ft/1.8m.

Cistus × purpureus (E) Many cistus need wall-shelter; this one deserves it most for its comparative tenderness and extravagant beauty. Rich dark pink blooms with maroon inner stains; these last only a day but replacement flowers shower the plant for a month. Grey-green leaves. To 6ft/1.8m high and wide. If you want a white cistus, try *C. aguilari* 'Maculatus' with crimson blotches: or *C.* 'Paladin', nearly semi-double.

Clematis The indispensable climber; notably in the form of the huge white 'Mme Le Coultre' (syn. 'Maire Boisselot') (A); 'Vyvyan Pennell' with double mauve rosettes (D); the

Charming pastel combination for semi-shade of Hydrangea anomala petiolaris *and* Clematis *'Hagley Hybrid', whose flowers bleach less out of sun.*

velvet garnet 'Niobe' (B); the large single violet-mauve 'Elsa Späth' (D) with a prolonged season of bloom'; the soft pink 'Hagley Hybrid' (C) will continue into autumn. 10ft/3m.

Cytisus battandieri The Moroccan Broom with spikes of yellow flowers smelling like ripe pineapples and even resembling them. Silky silver trifoliate leaves. Vigorous shrub to 13ft/4m and as wide.

Fremontodendron 'California Glory' (Semi-E) Large golden saucer flowers against three-lobed leaves, felted beneath with rusty down. For shelter, full sun, sandy and well-drained soil. 13ft × 8ft/4m × 2.4m: this shrub can be larger if not cut hard by frost.

Hydrangea anomala petiolaris Self-clinging climber for shade; a slow-starter, subsequently vigorous. 6in/15cm corymbs of creamy lacy flowers foam over its dense cover of bright green foliage. When young, tie in new shoots until their adhesive pads take over the work. 20ft/6m.

Lonicera (honeysuckle) in variety is desirable for its scent though none is easy against walls because of infestation by aphids. *L. × americana* makes a tremendous early show of cream and purple flowers (20ft/6m); *L. periclymenum* 'Belgica' has deep purple red fading to yellow inflorescences, whilst *L.p.* 'Serotina' flowers later (both 12ft/3.6m); the scentless coppery *L. × tellmaniana* needs moist soil and part shade (12ft/3.6m); and the glamour-puss of the lot, *L. tragophylla*, also scentless, has very large lemon flowers. Full shade. 32ft/10m.

Roses Any checklist of outstanding varieties must include the rambler 'Sanders' White' with cascading clusters of small scented flowers, once-blooming and late (14ft/4m); 'Seagull' (rambler) an earlier snowstorm of white single blossoms with golden stamens (20ft/6m); 'Madame Alfred Carrière' with large double blush-white heads, flowering with some recurrence (20ft/6m); 'Climbing Iceberg' with large luminous white blooms produced with great continuity (20ft/6m); 'Madame Grégoire Staechelin', in early summer extravagantly large rich pink frilly flowers with a scent to swoon by (20ft/6m); 'Constance Spry', once-flowering, large stuffed globular pink blooms, scented of myrrh, on a loose shrub which is spectacular trained on a wall (9ft/2.7m); the double shell-pink 'New Dawn', apple-scented, very recurrent, shiny-leafed and healthy (12ft/3.6m); 'Mermaid' with great sulphur yellow, amber-stamened single blossoms produced continuously and shining foliage (no pruning and must have shelter; 30ft/9m). Good soil and sun for all, though 'Mermaid' will tolerate part-shade.

Schizophragma integrifolium Rather like *Hydrangea anomala petiolaris*, but trickier. Its flower-heads which can be 12in/30cm across are surrounded by a number of showy white bracts. Tolerates shade. Self-clinging to 40ft/12m.

Solanum crispum 'Glasnevin' (Semi-E) Scandent shrub which needs wire support or a glamorous rose over which it can scramble. Its rich violet flowers with a central golden beak are produced in clusters all summer long. Full sun; very fast to 16ft/5m.

Late Summer to Autumn

Campsis x *tagliabuana* 'Madame Galen' A climber with pinnate leaves and very showy large poached salmon and red trumpets in terminal clusters. Needs support, full sun, shelter and pruning every spring. 20ft/6m.

Ceanothus The best and hardiest of the late-flowering evergreen varieties is 'Autumnal Blue'. The colour is soft but the massed effect from the panicles is strong; 8ft/2.4m. Of the deciduous cultivars, 'Gloire de Versailles' with large panicles is the most popular but the powder-blue is insipid (7ft/2.1m); try instead the deeper 'Topaz' which is tenderer. Full sun and a lightish soil.

Clematis Varieties of *C. viticella* are indispensable, such as 'Etoile Violette' with 3in/7.5cm purple saucers; 'Elvan' with nodding violet heads, tremendously flori-ferous; the velvety red 'Kermesina'; 'Abundance' with little wine-red nodding butterfly flowers; the white 'Alba Luxurians' its sepals

tipped sometimes with green; and the old double purple *C. v.* 'Purpurea Plena Elegans', covered in rosettes. All are vigorous, healthy, resistant to the scourge of wilt and tolerant of some shade. Height depends on whether you prune them in early spring (C or D). The best of the large-flowered hybrids must include the velvet purple 'Gypsy Queen' (15ft/4.6m); the pale blue 'Perle d'Azur' (12ft/3.6m). For a yellow scheme, include *C. tangutica* 'Bill Mackenzie' with ferny leaves and thick-textured yellow nodding lanterns, followed by silky silvery seed-heads. For sun; 20ft/6m. (All C).

Cotoneaster horizontalis Tough, common but valuable shady wall shrub where it will push and lean its way up the surface. Its fish-bone arrangement of branches, tiny leaves which redden in autumn and scarlet berries make it distinctive. 10ft/3m.

Escallonia 'Iveyi' (E) Choice tenderish shrub with showy panicles of small white flowers against dark toothed foliage. Vigorous but must have a warm sunny wall and good drainage; 8ft/2.4m.

Itea ilicifolia (E) has an air of sophistication with its 12in/30cm fragrant iced-green catkins shown to good effect against its dark glossy leaves. Sunny wall but moist soil. In mild areas can reach 15ft/4.6m, but the shrub is usually less.

Lathyrus latifolius (Everlasting Pea) Easy perennial climber making fresh growth each summer. It will ramble through plants or can be tied to supports. Both the purple-pink form and the glistening milky 'White Pearl' (which must have full sun) are lovely with bronze foliage. Annual growth to 8ft/2.4m.

Parthenocissus henryana Ornamental vine whose shoots will need some support; silver-veined dark green three- or five-lobed leaves which go maroon and ruby in autumn. Semi-shade and lovely with pink or white lacecap hydrangeas. 10ft/3m plus.

Passiflora caerulea The hardiest of the passion flowers is a woody climber which may act as a perennial after a hard winter. Its 4in/10cm white flowers are bossed with blue filaments and mass the plant. The ivory form 'Constance Elliott' is very lovely; so are new mauve hybrids but their hardiness is not yet

ABOVE: *A floriferous and new form of* Clematis viticella *called 'Elvan'.*

BELOW: Itea ilicifolia *produces its long fragrant catkins in summer.*

tested. Shelter, full sun. 15ft/4.6m.

Trachelospermum asiaticum (E) Self-clinging climber with clusters of 1in/2.5cm fragrant white flowers; small dark glossy leaves give dense coverage. It is hardier than *T. jasminoides*. Sun and shelter. 20ft/6m.

Vitis *V. vinifera* 'Purpurea' has stubby clusters of bitter black grapes late in the year by when its leaves have turned from their new sage-green, through maroon to near black. 15ft/4.6m. *V.* 'Brandt' is green-leafed until autumn when it is streaked with scarlet and gold; it, too, produces black grapes and makes a stunning screen over a trellis. Both have twining tips but will need some tying in for anchorage. 20ft/6m. *V. coignetiae* is the giant with which to sledgehammer tower blocks – 12in/30cm furrowed green leaves, crimsoning in autumn. Tie it to wires though its tendrils will do some clinging. 30ft/9m.

LEFT: *Even a low hedge arouses curiosity about the plants beyond it. The partially hidden is always enticing.*

OPPOSITE: *Brilliant treatment of the low wall to a water garden, lit up by a veneer of the blue Cedrus atlantica 'Glauca'.*

green feathery relative, S. *neapolitana*, bloom. The dying flower-stems will spoil the outline of the plant. This is also true of the emerald green S. *rosmarinifolia* (syn. S. *virens*) which is a lovely hedging plant. None of the above is long-lived, and the hedges will have to be continually renewed with cuttings taken in readiness against an early demise.

If it is true permanence you are after, the dwarf box, *Buxus sempervirens* 'Suffruticosa', is the answer though it is an expensive hedge as it has to be planted at 6in/15cm intervals. It gives the trimmest effect to a garden and, when crisply clipped (once or twice each summer), its geometric shape is the ultimate organizer.

LOW WALLS AND HEDGES

L ow walls are usually more versatile than high walls: they serve more purposes and therefore take different forms. They can retain vertical or sloping banks, make an architectural flank between service features like steps, or divide areas of the garden without screening one from another. They make dry wall gardens, form sunken gardens or, conversely, provide raised beds which save the owner from bending to flower borders on the ground.

Low hedges are especially valuable dividers of space, whether they are planned in a pattern themselves (as in knot gardens) or simply used to define the boundaries of a bed or a whole area. Lav-

ender is a favourite for hedging because of its scent, nostalgic associations, and ability to turn purple during the summer when it blooms. Also, its informality is a virtue in many contexts where constant clipping would be a burden to the gardener. Bear in mind, however, that informality is a euphemism for untidiness during half the year, since the flowering stems are better left untrimmed until spring. This makes for six months of tattiness.

Cotton lavender, the grey *Santolina chamaecyparissus*, looks much neater, since it is kept trimmed as a hedge throughout the season. Don't let this or its prettier grey-

The Retaining Wall

T he retaining wall provides the opportunity for one of the prettiest forms of gardening. What usually happens is that a bank has to be supported by a wall. In some circumstances, this means that the gardener can establish a border above it which weeps forward over the wall. Lovelier still, he may be able to plant at its

Dense planting on a series of raised beds with low walls is echoed by the high wall in the rear.

'Blue Mound' for early summer. The semi-horizontal junipers will also provide evergreen cover; but, being a bit dull and ubiquitous, they might be enlivened with the less vigorous trailers of the clematis tribe. Silvery artemisias like *A. canascens*, looking like filigree silver wire, or the glittering evergrey *A.* 'Powis Castle' will add light to a scheme.

The Dry Wall

Often small rather than large effects are desirable: maybe space is very limited or you want to introduce the diminutive perfection of alpines. In this case, walls that retain banks can be used to grow rock plants. The rule of thumb when planting these is that they should look natural. The flowers must appear comfortable and the effect uncontrived. Ideally, the stone should be or appear to be natural. Visible mortar, even at a weak point, is an abomination. Soil and compost only should fill the joints of the wall.

The ideal method is to plant as the wall is built. There are three good reasons for this. One, you can insert plump and well root-balled plants. Two, you can bed them as satisfactorily as you could in a border on the ground, spreading the roots out and watering them into their new home. Three, they are likely to thrive and not perish – a likely outcome of trying to squeeze them into a space in an existing wall.

foot, in which case he relates the plants vertically – for those at the bottom must be suitable companions for those visible in the border above. This kind of border-topped wall is often seen in gardens built on steep hillsides which are flowery paradises formed out of terraces.

What do you plant at the top of the wall? Ideally, mound-forming plants which spray forwards and hang over the retaining wall. Arching low roses like 'Raubritter' with its pink globular shells; the semi-prostrate broom, *Cytisus* × *kewensis* with its skirts of cream flowers in spring; the azure hummocks of the evergreen *Ceanothus*

Selecting Plants

The kind of plant you choose depends partly on the wall's aspect (sunny or shady), partly on the degree of moisture it can provide, and partly on the plant's habit of growth. Ideally you want a picturesque balance between those plants that tuft up erectly, those that hang down like neat goatee beards, and those with a more spreading patriarchal growth. Evergreen leaves are an advantage, a range of different flowering seasons usually an essential. Your aim is to achieve a satisfying picture made up of trailers and creepers, flowers and foliage, cushion-forming mounds, shrubby plants and so forth.

More than aesthetics comes into the positioning of the plants. The flowers make their own demands. Most bulbs and tenderish plants need a drier position; these will have to go near the top of the wall. But those that want a moist root run – any primulas or ferns, for example – must go near the bottom or at the foot. It follows that these walls give you the chance to grow a tremendously wide range of plants.

They also open the door to growing flowers which could scarcely be tried in other positions. An example would be alpines with woolly leaves or with vulnerable crowns whose foliage or centres are liable to rot when grown horizontally where they will collect rainwater. Instead, they need to be grown vertically, where rain reaches them but cannot settle and stagnate on their vulnerable parts. The *Lewisia* genus is one example.

Other types of miffy plants include the floriferous blue or white trailing *Campanula isophylla*, the fluorescent magenta *Calandrinia umbellata*; the blue *Convolvulus sabatius* and its rich pink relative *C. altheoides*. Winter frosts would probably knock all these out in another less protected or drained position. In a sunny dry wall, they stand a chance of surviving in cool temperate climates.

Clematis montana rubens on a fence fronting the road is allowed to drip down to the clouds of aubrieta on the stone wall beneath it.

Plants for Sunny Walls
(Measurements denote spread or fall)

Acaena if carefully selected, make useful carpeters on the flat and trailers on walls. Avoid those which creep invasively and will infest a whole wall in the end. *A.* 'Blue Haze' is one of the best though very vigorous, putting out long woody trails, covered with tiny blue-grey foliage. Its crimson burrs in summer will self-seed unless cut off; 3ft/90cm.

Aethionema 'Warley Rose' is a bushy plant with thin dark leaves and terminal clusters of pink flowers in early summer. It will grow to about 12in/30cm high and wide on a wall.

Alyssum saxatile is the most popular wall plant despite the harsh brassiness of its gold in spring. The variety *A.s. citrinum* is a softer lemon though a weaker grower. Growth to 2ft/60cm.

Androsace lanuginosa makes a summer crinoline of blush flower-heads, each tiny blossom with a ruby central point – a shower of bloom over trailing silvery-green foliage. 18in/45cm.

Aubrieta is the inevitable purple companion to alyssum in spring. Vigorous and smothering, its best forms include the rich violet 'Dr. Mules' and the self-explanatory 'Rose Cascade' and 'Red Cascade'. 2ft/60cm.

Campanula in variety, from the enthusiastic *C. poscharskyana* with blue stars (2ft/60cm), to the rather less vigorous *C. garganica*, with pale lavender-blue stars. *C. cochlearifolia* has little white or blue down-turned thimbles making an enchanting effect, but its roots are invasive. *C. portenschlagiana* has deeper violet-blue bells and makes a stunning hanging mat to 18in/45cm. All summer flowering.

Lithodora diffusa is for acid soils only. It will make a large evergreen mat over a wall, perpetually in flower, a dazzling rich blue. Selected forms include 'Heavenly Blue' and 'Grace Ward'. Spreading to 3ft/90cm where happy.

Phlox subulata makes a hanging evergreen mat. A variety of hybrids provide a range of colour from magenta to white, lilac, blue or violet in late spring. 'Oakington Blue' has sky blue flowers; 'Emerald Cushion' has lilac; up

A retaining wall, heightened by a hedge. Berberis on the top of the wall coordinates with Alyssum saxatile *beneath it.*

to 2ft/60cm. *P.douglasii* is not usually quite so vigorous; 'Daniel's Cushion' has large rich pink blossoms.

Saponaria ocymoides has small bright pink flowers smothering the plant in summer. Cascading, fast and very easy. 2½ft/75cm.

Plants for Shady Walls

Arenaria balearica is a vigorous dark evergreen mat-former with a starring of tiny white flowers in spring and summer. For acid soils where it will spread to 4ft/1.2m.

Chiastophyllum oppositifolium Distinctive golden tassels in early summer in sun or shade over green rosettes; 12in/30cm. A

Chiastophyllum oppositifolium *produces its clear yellow tassels in early summer and tolerates sun or shade.*

Primula auricula *is easy to raise from seed and ideal for the shady side of the wall; in sun, it will need more moisture.*

lovely companion for the little black-leafed purple-flowered *Viola labradorica purpurea* which flowers at the same time though starting earlier. This will seed all over the wall, but is always pretty.

Codonopsis clematidea is a trailing herbaceous charmer for an eye-level wall where you can see its dark interior rings within its icy blue bells in summer; 18in/45cm high and wide.

Ferns, especially the evergreen *A. trichomanes* with its wiry black stems and fine leaves; 6in/15cm. The Hart's-Tongue Fern, *Phyllitis scolopendrium*, is a more assertive broad-leafed fern for focal points, with shining green fronds. There are crimped and crested forms for fun, but they are no

artistic improvement on the simple outline of the type. 18in/45cm.

Fragaria vesca 'Variegata' is a very showy strawberry with cream and grey-green leaves; cream saucer flowers in early summer. Good for a dark corner but can root around the wall invasively; 18in/45cm but infinite spread.

Omphalodes verna Little intensely blue flowers in spring on dark green mats; a running habit to 18in/45cm or more.

Ramonda myconi Choice and enchanting with mauve flowers, centering on a gold beak, in late spring over rosettes of puckered rough green leaves. One of those plants which will rot if rain collects in its rosette, so it must be tucked into the wall so that its leaves are parallel with its surface. 12in/30cm.

ABOVE: *A sunny aspect ensures a good display from plants that perform late in the year.*

RIGHT: *Meconopsis is amongst the most beautiful flowers for a shady border but it will only thrive in an acid soil with a high humus content.*

BORDERS AGAINST WALLS

A picturesque wall is an asset in itself. Even any wall or fence will provide you with the dual value of its shady and sunny surface for your plants. However, a wall is exploitable for more than itself. It also offers you the chance to develop a sunny and a shady border within its lee.

The sunny border receives a double baking, not only by the sun but by the reflected heat from the wall behind it. Wood and buds ripen, flower production improves, frost is less likely to take effect on any sappy shoot tips and flowers. Half-hardy perennials will bloom for longer; late-performers like many chrysanthemums will perform better.

Even a shady border by a wall – though always cooler than its obverse – can still enjoy some of the same shelter. Unless circumstances are exceptional, scourging wind or prolonged freezing in winter will have less effect. Powdery snow will admittedly pile up in drifts against a wall border, when the wind blows it around. But this only serves to protect the underlying plants against the worst ravages of cold: they are safely tucked beneath a blanket until it melts.

Planting Lime-intolerant Subjects

The only situation in which walls and plants might not mix is when you use subjects that cannot tolerate lime – shrubs like rhododendrons, camellias, leptospermums and many herbaceous plants. This can be tricky: camellias, for example, are just the sort of desirable early-flowering shrubs whose blooms one

wants to protect in a sheltered situation.

You are only likely to encounter this problem if limy mortar in your wall has leached into the soil beneath. (If your wall is actually limestone, then you shouldn't be growing any lime-intolerant plants at all.) In this case, make up a lime-free compost in which to plant, the details of which are given on page 58. Where you have reason to suspect that leakage of lime may be continuous, you may have to put a polythene lining between the wall and the soil. Use a thick-grade sheeting so that your efforts endure.

Designing Wall Borders

This is much easier than designing an island border. You have a firm architectural backdrop for all your efforts. You have a stage. You need only present its front to the world. However, thin borders need a different approach from expansive borders. House borders must be planned on a taller scale than garden wall borders. And hedge borders may well contain a separate range of plants from those used beside masonry walls. Each has its own problems of design as the following pages illustrate.

THE HOUSE WALL BORDER

Planting up the house wall border is not without problems. The trouble is that you are not starting with a blank canvas but a fidgety one. On a house façade you have any number of windows not all of which may be of uniform size or style. You also have doors and, perhaps, even balconies which are excrescences on the wall before you begin pouring on plants.

With a very fussy or small house façade, the only satisfactory approach to planting is to opt for a bold simplicity: maybe a single long horizontal garland of *Clematis montana*; a glossy covering of scented white *Magnolia grandiflora*; the romantic extravagance of wisteria. With a simple large façade, you can opt for more varieties, but try to make links between them so that

---

A house wall can be problematic to plant, for walls, porches, access, style of building must all be taken into account. In this admirable example, the house appears to grow out of its garden – one is inseparable from the other yet does not interfere. The mauve Solanum crispum grows up the façade with wisteria beyond. A tapestry of euphorbias, cistus, ballota and sisyrinchium clothes the base.

they present a homogeneous effect. And, when working out the position for different climbers, remember too that some of the excrescences on house walls need concealing rather than avoiding. One example is the downpipe for which an evergreen climber can be useful.

Plants in the House Wall Border

Many climbers growing in this position have bare and lanky legs because they are so tall. They also have thick ankles when they are mature. The result is that they tend to show their attractions (their top-knot of flowers) at a slight distance; whereas their ugly lower parts are the more apparent when you are nearby. What you can do here is to plant secondary climbers over your main hosts, allowing their flexible trailers to hang down over the hosts' legs. And even a narrow border at their base can be filled with plants which are solid, shrubby and evergreen. Measures like this will go a long way towards redeeming the defects of the biggest climbers.

Even narrow borders beside a house can accommodate plants of different heights. What you are assembling here is a flattened version of the big border with the tall ones (the climbers) at the back and the little edgers at the front. However, the very fact that you are condensing the levels means that you will have tall and small mixed in.

Don't forget bulbs here which take so little room and give so much return in a small space. You might choose those which will rise up through the foliage of low bushy plants to a mid-level. Perhaps Crown Imperials (*Fritillaria imperialis*), loveliest against a wall which protects them against bad weather at the time they bloom. Or a 2ft/60cm allium like *A. christophii* with its giant heads of lilac stars. Avoid very tall bulbs whether alliums or lilies. In this position these will lean forward as they grow, like suspended guardsmen about to faint but never actually capitulating.

Problems beside Houses

Planting conditions are likely to be extreme beside a house. The soil is either terribly dry as the eaves block the rainfall; conversely, stagnant damp may be the trouble – a dripping gutter without a soakaway is a likely culprit. In this case, plant horses for courses. Shady dry conditions are the most challenging. Try the ever-tolerant *Cotoneaster horizontalis* on the wall, with a floor of *Vinca minor* 'Aureo-variegata' with gold and green leaves and white star flowers. Or the shrubby climber *Euonymus* 'Silver Queen' can be used with pale blue and white pulmonarias and *Brunnera macrophylla* with its showers of azure forget-me-not flowers.

THE GARDEN WALL BORDER

A decorative wall of choice architecture needs sensitive planting. Leaves, flowers and the picturesque highlights of the masonry must share their space to mutual advantage. A humdrum wooden fence needs, in contrast, total obliteration – climbing roses, fanned out to encourage flowering, vines, clematis, and frequent evergreens so that in winter its nudity will be less drab.

Trellis is best adorned with scrambling, twining and tendrilled climbers which are flexible enough to slip in and out of its holes – jasmine, clematis, solanum, vines. Add honeysuckles and rambling roses whose long shoots are more pliant than those of climbers. These are also more likely to thrive in the airy conditions of open trelliswork than on solid walls which make them succumb to mildew and aphids.

Most garden walls are no more than 6ft/1.8m. No climber worth its name is going to reach its natural ultimate height vertically here, so it will have to spread its growth semi-horizontally. This can look tremendously effective backing a border. A single rose, for example, may extend for 20ft/6m along a wall, giving you a uniform backdrop for a variety of plants that you place before it. United by their common background, they will appear much more cohesive than might otherwise be the case.

Clematis macropetala 'Maidwell Hall' contrasts with Euphorbia characias wulfenii.

The Unity of Wall and Border

Cohesion is always essential between the plantings on wall and border. Backdrop and foreground are kin here. You can achieve this most obviously by relating the flower colours on each – whether by contrast or by compatibility. You can also let the climbing plants on the wall bush forward or become lightly entwined with the plants beside them, as with the clematis and the euphorbia in the photograph. Or you can build a careful assembly of foliage effects so that vertical and horizontal layers form a single picture.

In addition you should plan to integrate tall border plants so that they are on the same level as the climbers. The worst kind of wall border has tall verticals on the wall and low flat horizontal plants in the border before it. Neither shakes hands. You can avoid this absurdity by deliberately including tall growers like hollyhocks, the silver cut-leafed globe artichokes or cardoons, the larger verbascums and the silver spiny onopordons. Plant them a little way out from the wall to

An effective association of foliage: wisteria, Euonymus 'Silver Queen' and Santolina neapolitana (both evergreen).

Bourbon rose with nepeta softens the reddish tones of the brick wall.

minimize their tendency to lean towards the light.

Problems beside the Garden Wall

Like the house wall, dryness may be a difficulty when planting beside the solid fence or garden wall. Whilst there are no eaves to contend with, it is likely that one side of the wall (the other side from the prevailing wind, probably) will be in the rain shadow. Moreover, the sunny side of a masonry wall and its foundations are going to dry out rapidly and bake in summer.

Most climbers will cope with this if they are suitably chosen for their site and the ground is well-prepared and regularly nourished and mulched subsequently. But if this is difficult or the soil is very shallow, consider using certain drought- and heat-tolerant shrubs and training them as climbers. You can do this, for example, with the taller cistus – the loveliest, C × purpureus, carmine with maroon stains, would look gorgeous beside the silver, silky, feathery Artemisia arborescens. Both are tender; both will benefit from the shelter of being trained back against the wall.

49

THE HEDGE BORDER

The foot of a hedge is not so easy a planting position as a wall. The soil is bound to be robbed of nutrients whatever the nature of the hedge, and quite apart from its lack of nourishment, is going to be dry. Any choice of plant is going to need a degree of personal attention to thrive.

Climbers

You cannot adorn a hedge with a climber whose period of growth is going to interfere with the hedge clipping. So any hedge that needs clipping two or three times a year (a myrobalan or *Lonicera nitida*, for example) is an unsuitable host for a climber. That is a practical consideration. An aesthetic one is the look of the hedge. A big-leafed variety like laurel is too obtrusive. What you want is a dark, tiny-leafed hedge which will be a background cloth to your climber. Yew is the obvious ideal; it also needs clipping only once and not until late in the year.

On its sunny side, you can plant climbing annual nasturtiums which will bloom better in the poor soil beside the greedy yew, sending their fiery velvet flowers up through the twigs in the latter part of the summer. On the shady side, the classic adornment is the related hardy and perennial *Tropaeolum speciosum*; blooming from summer into the autumn, its crimson velvet flowers will cascade in garlands over the hedge – but it will only thrive if you ensure it is kept moist and nourished in humus-rich soil. Very much a case of personal attention.

The rhizomatous Tropaeolum speciosum grown on the shady side of a yew hedge. It thrives better in cool moist regions and will put out annual growth to 6ft/1.8m.

This hedge has been planted and trimmed to form armchair wings making extra snug compartments for a seat and plants.

The Thin Hedge-Border

In sun, bulbs should do well here as they need a summer baking and the spring-flowering ones especially will appreciate a little shelter at this windy time of year. A ribbon of daffodils is always simple, easy and charming – try the pale varieties like 'Ice Follies' or the white and frilly, orange-centred double 'Flower Drift'. Add to these crocus, scillas, chionodoxa, muscari and some tulip species. The latest-flowering tulip, *Tulipa sprengeri*, scarlet and buff, glows like a jewel beside a purple hedge like *Berberis thunbergii atropurpurea* or copper beech.

Where a hedge is on a bank, you need a smotherer to cover the bank, but tougher taller bulbs can still grow through it. Try the green-and cream-leafed *Vinca major* 'Variegata' with large blue-violet flowers in spring, but let white narcissi and golden daffodils push up amongst it.

Hedge Bottoms in Shade

In this position, any of the following should be fairly tolerant: the yellow starry-flowered *Allium moly*, the violet *Viola labradorica purpurea*, the carpeter *Waldsteinea ternata* with its yellow strawberry flowers, and *Alchemilla mollis* with its lime-yellow showers. Evergreen pulmonarias, vincas and the tolerant evergreen *Iris foetidissima variegata* with its cream striped leaves and husks of orange berries from autumn onwards are all decorative and reliable companions.

Buttresses and their Beds

Finally don't forget that hedges which have the luxury of ornamental buttresses can hold a series of individual beds. Flanked on three sides, the plants are sheltered and snug. Simple schemes are the best here: blue forget-me-nots and pink and white lily-flowering tulips for spring; glowing hemerocallis for summer; hellebores for winter.

THE LARGE WALL-BACKED BORDER

The large wall-backed mixed border is the horticultural set-piece of any garden. The prototype, a huge herbaceous border backed by a yew hedge, was probably made in England in the 1840s at Arley Hall in Cheshire.

This 'invention' proved an ideal way of displaying plants though it was challenged in the 1950s when the island border was popularized. To me, the latter has three damning faults. One, it

leads to the restless fussiness of beds popping up all over the place, there being no raison d'être for one position over another. Two, plants in any moderately exposed garden suffer from the lack of an immediately sheltering wall or hedge. Three, all plants lack shape or look untidy for part of the year and need an architectural form to set them off. A wall or formal hedge gives them the necessary anchorage and frame. An island bed doesn't.

Leaning to the Light

Aesthetically the case for the big walled border is easily proven. How does it rate from the practical point of view? Does it need extra staking? The problem lies in the fact that plants nearest the wall are drawn by a lack of light behind them and need support. The deeper the border, the less the light. Gertrude Jekyll devised a cure for this problem in her own huge border at Munstead Wood. She built a narrow alley between the plants and the wall which provided access to the wall shrubs at the back of the border. A contrivance of this kind is

RIGHT: *Sympathetic colouring between border and wall planting makes one flow into the other for maximum impact. Lythrum salicaria 'Robert' is backed by mauve clematis with golden hop (top left) for contrast.*
OPPOSITE: *A wall-backed herbaceous border on the right is improved by being given its twin border forming a stongly directional path.*

some help towards letting light into the back of a border and therefore reducing the need of staking for support.

Luxuriance in the Border

I t is luxuriance of growth that the large wall-border is best designed to provide. When you add the height of the wall or fence which is perhaps 6ft/1.8m or more to the depth of the bed – which should be a minimum of 6ft/1.8m too – then the sum total is a large surface area to support plants.

In a space of this kind nothing shows up so disadvantageously as thin contents or proportions. This kind of border has got to billow forth and billow it won't if the plants are too insubstantial, too short on the ground or too flat on the wall. Wall and border should be a great homogeneous waterfall of flowers and foliage where, in parts at least, one surface can scarcely be unpicked from the other.

This sense of luxuriance will evaporate if you don't treat the extremities in the same way. You want plants

to spill lavishly over the front of the border rather than stopping short of the edge; they should be a fair match for all those wall plants.

Disciplines of Form and Colour

A ll this talk of generosity doesn't mean that the disciplines of form and

colour can be forgotten. Loss of control means chaos here as anywhere else in a garden. Allow the wall to show through at points so that the nature of this border isn't entirely submerged under vegetable life. And discipline your colours so that you can build up related effects through each layer of the border, from front to back and from top to bottom.

53

A potager can be glimpsed through a young espalier fruit screen.

THE KITCHEN GARDEN

In a small garden especially, the space for a kitchen garden is at a premium. What often happens is that flowers and fruit have to be integrated. Though a necessity, it can be made a virtue if the garden is designed to this end. However, if plants are to thrive – kitchen produce most of all – they need space and light around them. One way of ensuring that fruit enjoys these conditions is to grow it on walls and fences. Here, its limbs can be spread out to form espaliers, lifted diagonally into cordons which are space-savers, or – the pretty one but very time-consuming – laid out into delicate fans, each stem and sub-lateral making a vein of the fan. Although these modes require careful training, they will make a garden look spruce automatically. And in blossom as well as fruit, all fruit trees look idyllically beautiful.

Bringing order and pattern into the garden may be one advantage. There are practical purposes too. Some trees need their blossom sheltered against frost if they flower early. Other fruit will only ripen adequately against a warm wall. Moreover, fruit which is likely to be stripped by birds, is much more easily protected by netting against a wall than when grown in the open, in which case you need to provide a virtual cage.

Brick walls provide the ideal conditions for fruit-growing, because the bricks are porous enough to absorb and retain warmth. But a soft stone runs it close and I am always impressed how the porous old red sandstone of my walls emits heat even on a chilly evening after any warm day. However, any wall is better than none. And if you don't have a wall at all? Then you can turn hardy fruit into a wall in itself by growing it as an espalier fruit screen. This can make a charming division across a garden, and requires no more than posts and strained wires.

A finishing touch is to plant suitably at the foot of the wall fruits. This adds a neat detail which makes for a very decorative effect. Don't plant right under the tree when it is established, however, as you will probably disturb the roots; cherry trees in particular may pack in the struggle. Try to do this when you plant or when the trees are young and their roots haven't explored their area.

Avoid anything greedy that is going to rob the tree of its nourishment. Bulbs are fine, and, if the wall is sunny, choose those that will need a summer baking: tulips (though not those that will need lifting after flowering); for autumn, pink amaryllis and nerines; for late winter, the rhizomatous mauve *Iris unguicularis*. For shady walls, instead of bulbs, you could use the little alpine strawberry for food as well as ornament.

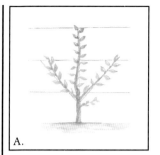

A.

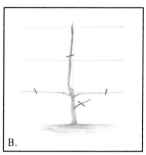

B.

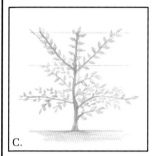

C.

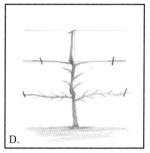

D.

Training for an Espalier Screen

Plant maiden trees (one-year olds) at 10 – 20ft/ 3 – 6m apart, depending on rootstock and space. Prune to 2in/5cm above the bottom training wire, above three buds at the top, two pointing outwards in opposite directions. The top bud will grow up, continuing the main stem. The side ones will grow out; you will train these eventually along the horizontal wires.
A. As these side shoots develop the next season, tie them to diagonal canes.
B. In early winter, lower and attach them to the bottom horizontal wire, trimming the weak growth by a third or less. Prune the upright stem to above the second hori- zontal wire as originally and cut the little side branches to three buds.
C. The next summer, train the second branches as in (A). In later summer, prune shoots from small branches on the trunk and also branchlets produced on the two bottom main branches to about three leaves beyond the basal leaf cluster.
D. In early winter, the third horizontal tier is treated in the same way as the previous tiers. Assuming there are only three espalier wires, in the following summer cut the top of the trunk back to the top wire. Thereafter, as the branches begin to fill the length of their wires, trim them back each winter. Prune growth on the trunk and branches to three leaves beyond the basal leaf cluster.

Fruits for Different Aspects

There is room for flexibility over which fruit you grow on which wall, but not on the sunniest wall. In cool regions the following fruit trees will need it.

FOR FULL SUN

Apricot This is grown as a fan usually. Cultivars are self-fertile but the fact that they bloom in the chilly part of the year means they need shelter in cold snaps and you should pollinate them by hand. Tie a scut of cotton-wool on a short stick and touch each flower with it. Plant at a distance of 18 – 24ft/ 5.5 – 7.5m.

Figs Highly decorative with glossy architectural leaves. Usually fan-trained to allow the fruit to ripen. Self-fertile and grown on its own root-stock which should be restricted in a bed of 2½ft/75cm. In cold regions, protect the branches of the fig (the tips bear next year's crop). Plant 13 – 20ft/ 4 – 6m apart.

Grapevines These can be grown as cordons or espaliers and in either case will occupy a lot of space unless strictly checked. Choose a variety whether green or black which the nurseryman knows will fruit satisfactorily in your area. Planting distance will depend on the method of growth.

Peaches and nectarines Both grown as fans and varieties of each are self-fertile. Protect against spring frosts and pollinate by hand. If the top growth is restricted, their planting distances don't need to be as large as the apricot's.

THE WALL WITH MORNING SUN

Apples Hardy, late-cropping varieties should fruit here and can be grown as espaliers. On the most dwarfing rootstock (only for a low wall), plant 10ft/3m apart; on semi-dwarfing, 12 – 15ft/3.6 – 4.6m apart; on vigorous, for large espaliers, add 3ft/90cm.

Pears are suitable here but if you have room for one fruit tree only, don't make it a pear as most lone pears cannot set fruit but need a

A fan-trained plum on a wall. The tulips at its feet are 'Keizerkroon' and T. clusiana which enjoy a summer baking.

Espaliered apple in blossom. The horizontal wires are about 1in/2.5cm from the wall to allow air to circulate.

mate to cross-pollinate them. Even 'Conference', a self-fertile cultivar, has inferior fruits when it is lonely. On a dwarfing rootstock, plant 12 – 15ft/3.6 – 4.6m apart, and add on 5ft/1.5m for a semi-vigorous rootstock.

WALL WITH AFTERNOON SUN
Choice dessert pears and dessert apples are at their best here (see rootstocks and planting distances above).
Sweet Cherries These will need netting against the birds which is more easily done against a wall than in the open. Fan-training is the traditional form of growth. On semi-vigorous rootstock, plant 12 – 15ft/3.6 – 4.6m apart and add 5ft/1.5m on vigorous.
Plums will do well in the warmth, including the traditional greengage with its rich flavour, dripping with juice. Ensure you have suitable varieties for cross-pollination if necessary though some cultivars (like 'Victoria') are self-fertile. Grown fan-trained usually. On a

semi-dwarfing rootstock, plant 15 – 18ft/ 4.6 – 5.6m apart.

THE SHADY WALL
Morello Cherry is the most commonly grown acid cherry in this position. It is ethereally lovely clothed in its fragile white blossom in spring and when jewelled with its dark red fruits later. Normally grown as a fan. On semi-vigorous fruit-stock, plant 12 – 15ft/3.6 – 4.6m apart.
Gooseberry The fruit is clearly visible on walls and you can pick it with ease. Train as a fan or a cordon; the latter can be single, double or triple and is planted about 2ft/60cm apart. Plant fans 4ft/1.2m apart. Prune in winter shortening the side shoots to three buds.
Redcurrant This is usually grown in single cordons spaced 1 – 1½/30 – 45cm apart. Net against birds. Hard prune in summer and winter to make the single stem fruitful.

PREPARING AND PLANTING

We ask a lot of wall plants. We want them to perform rapidly and to dazzling effect. Yet, often, they are squeezed for space, short of rain, sometimes even deprived of light. We grow them in layers, expecting two or three plants to thrive on top of one another, competing for room and nourishment. Is it surprising that few plants will amuse us for long unless we give them what they need?

The support system on which several plants (like this rose and clematis) are grown in layers has to be strong and durable.

Soil

What they need is good soil – not the gravel and builder's debris that is commonly their lot at the base of a wall. It may be necessary to replace all this with imported top soil to a depth of 18in/45cm. Compost, leaf mould, rotted straw, peat (or not, depending on your convictions) as well as rotted manure will also give a plant a good start. So will grit or extra coarse sand for drainage on heavy clay soils. Nutrients supplied by an organic manure (blood, fish and bone) or a balanced inorganic fertilizer can be lightly forked in at the time of planting and, in future years, applied in the early spring.

Ericaceae (such as camellias and rhododendrons) and other lime-intolerant plants are going to need a lime-free compost. Take out all trace of builder's debris and fill in with the kind of compost recommended for camellias: 7 parts by bulk of turfy acid loam, 3 parts of granulated sedge peat, 2 parts of gritty lime-free sand. To each bushel is added 1½oz/42gm of bonemeal and the same amount of coarse hoof and horn mixture.

When making a bed against a house, never raise it above the damp-proof course. Keep it 6in/15cm below.

Preparing the Wall or Fence

The support system for wall plants needs to be tough, particularly if you are growing one on top of another. If your plants are not reliably self-clinging, a high wind can detach and break not just one plant, but all the others which are on its back as well.

One of the most durable forms of support is strong galvanized wire stretched horizontally over the wall at intervals of 8 – 12in/20 – 30cm and held in position by stout eyelet-hole metal nails or galvanized hooks which have been driven into the wall or fence posts. In the case of a masonry wall, drill a hole and plug it for the nails to enter: they may bend and twist if you just hammer them into resistant mortar. You can also use pig netting (a very wide-gauge rust-resistant mesh), or wooden trellis, though this can look more obvious than the plants and is expensive.

Camellias need lime-free soil at the foot of a wall. If lime is in the mortar they will fail to thrive.

Planting

Pot-grown plants should have their root-balls thoroughly wetted before they are taken from their containers. Then gently loosen any tightly woven bottom roots before inserting the plant in its hole. Position it about 15in/37cm out from the base of the wall so that rain can reach it. It will still require steady watering at the beginning of its life and, probably, mulching in early spring thereafter.

Clematis require special treatment as a precaution against the common disease of wilt. Plant the root-ball 2in/5cm deeper than the soil level in the container. If the plant goes down with wilt, it will then have a chance to thrust up more shoots from below soil level. Always shade the roots, whether with a stone slab, thick mulch or another plant.

Serpentine hedge made of hornbeam. On the sunny side, its concave bays gather warmth.

PRUNING AND TRAINING

Pruning is important for wall plants which can become too unwieldy for their station, turning into horsehair mattresses in no time. However, not all pruning rules are written in stone, and commonsense and inertia may give you a year's inactivity without anything terrible happening.

Clematis The clematis varieties on pages 31 – 36 are given the codes A – D. For A, thin end shoots and tidy the plant lightly to the main framework after flowering. For B, in late winter/early spring, cut back by one-third all the growth made in the previous year. For C, in late winter/early spring, cut back all the previous year's growth to 1ft/30cm from the base. For D, no pruning is needed unless the clematis is overflowing its space. Often pruning is optional and you can adapt it to encourage flowering at a suitable time or height.

Roses Rambler roses are mostly unhappy against walls, where they are prone to mildew. The few exceptions can be pruned after flowering; remove dead shoots and cut back the flowering laterals to near the stem. Trim the leaders if necessary back to strong new growth. Climbing roses can be pruned when fully dormant. Do this on the wall or detach them from their supports and lay them on the ground (the winter winds may have conveniently done this for you). Trim the old

A dead tree doesn't always have to be removed from a wall. Covered with netting, it can be used as a host for a strong clematis like 'Perle d'Azur'.

Training

Roses flower best fanned into a diagonal to semi-horizontal formation. If grown vertically the sap tends to rush to the head and you lose the lower blossoms. Clematis is tricky; guide shoots gently to supports in the direction you want them to go. Shrubs can be free-standing or have their back shoots tied to the wall. All ties should be durable. Tarred string will collapse by the end of a season and the wind-rock on unfettered evergreens can be so great that huge branches will break off, bringing their wire support down with them from the wall. Pieces of nylon stocking are strong and won't chafe the stems.

Protection

Avoidance of disease is better than having to deal with it. Plant clematis in the way described on page 59 in case of wilt. Don't plant roses you know are prone to blackspot and rust in your area. Don't put honeysuckles on hot sunny walls where they are prone to aphids. Spraying any of these plants is horrible on a wall as you get showered with the stuff. In winter, protect tender plants with netting, lightly draped muslin curtains, or a skirt of straw at the base. It is on its lower regions that you depend for regrowth so make sure that your protection is not so dense it encourages rot-inducing moisture.

flowered shoots hard back to three buds. Cut out very old growth if necessary if you have strong new replacement growth as a substitute.
Vines Prune in mid-winter. If they are cut in summer their sap is liable to 'bleed'.
Flowering Shrubs These can bosom out too far. Trim those that blossom in the early part of the year (i.e. on old wood) immediately after flowering. Some like chaenomeles will flower better for being taken back to a few buds from the main stems and, for strict training, outward-pointing shoots should be removed. Shrubs that blossom after midsummer are flowering on new wood made in the current year. Prune these the following spring. With flowering and fruiting shrubs like pyracantha, you remove the berries when you cut off the flowering shoots. Divide the pruning between spring and autumn and do it lightly. Tender evergreens like ceanothus should be spring pruned and their outward-pointing shoots especially tipped. Never cut into their old wood. Don't prune cistus.

INDEX

Diana Saville is the author of six gardening books and the editor of Letts Guides to Garden Design. She has also been gardening correspondent of a national newspaper and has written widely for journals and magazines. Her previous books which have been published in America and Britain have earned her a high reputation.

    She has a country garden with an inner high walled courtyard and a number of small hedged enclosures, so she is especially fond of gardening with walls and screens.

PRINTED IN BELGIUM BY

proost
INTERNATIONAL BOOK PRODUCTION